MARCUS BONTEMPELLI

FOOTY LEGENDS

First published by Albert Street Books, an imprint of Allen & Unwin, in 2025

Allen & Unwin
Cammeraygal Country
83 Alexander Street
Crows Nest NSW 2065
Australia
Phone: (61 2) 8425 0100
Email: info@allenandunwin.com
Web: www.allenandunwin.com

Allen & Unwin acknowledges the Traditional Owners of the Country on which we live and work. We pay our respects to all Aboriginal and Torres Strait Islander Elders, past and present.

EU Authorised Representative: Easy Access System Europe, Mustamäe tee50, 10621 Tallinn, Estonia, gpsr.requests@easproject.com

A catalogue record for this book is available from the National Library of Australia

ISBN 978 1 76118 174 0

For teaching resources, explore allenandunwin.com/learn

Cover design by Hana Kinoshita Thomson
Cover photo by Quinn Rooney / Getty Images
Text design by Hana Kinoshita Thomson
Set in 14 pt Urbane Rounded Medium
Printed and bound in Australia by the Opus Group

10 9 8 7 6 5 4 3 2

KIT CROSS

LEIGH HEDSTROM

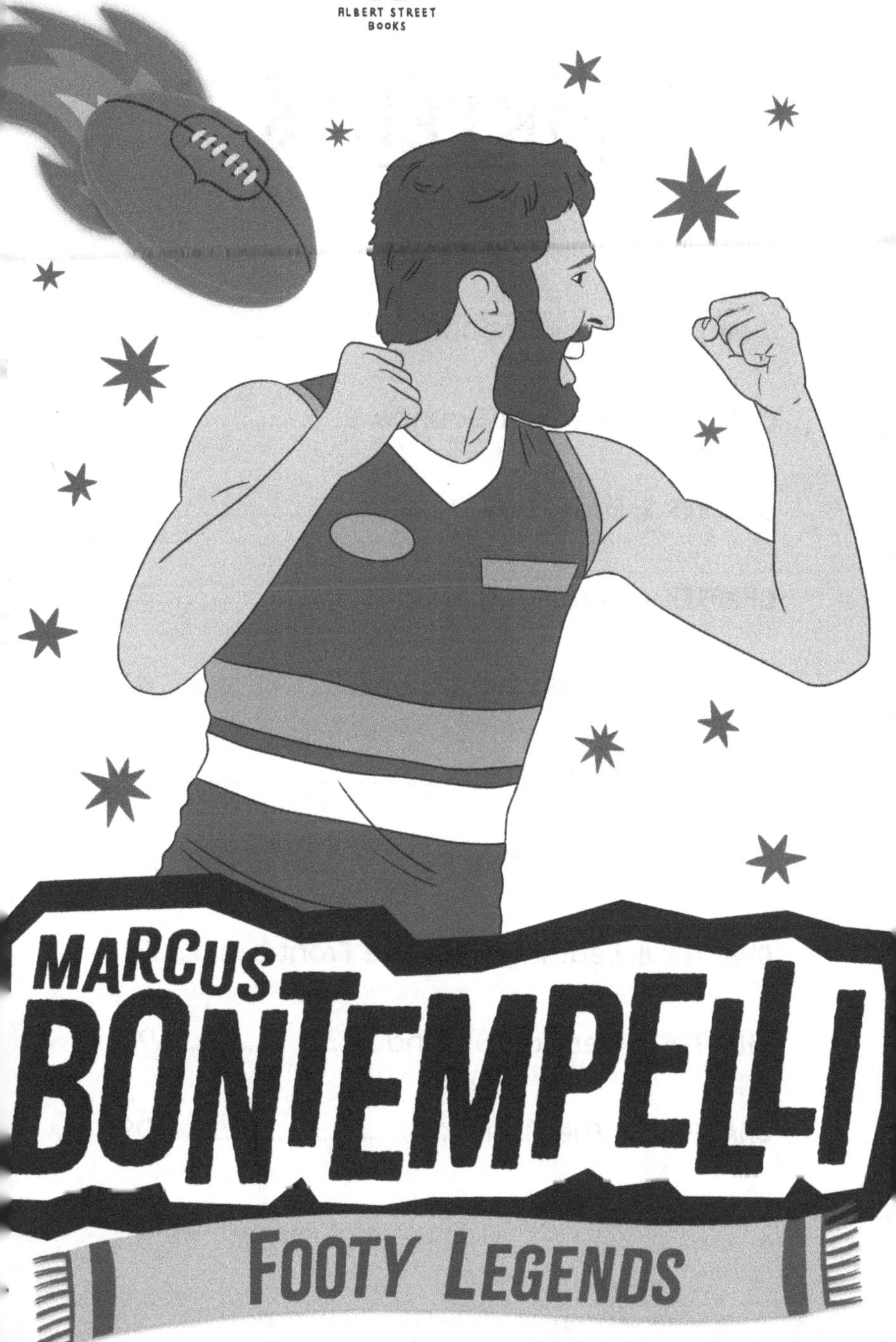

MARCUS BONTEMPELLI

FOOTY LEGENDS

CONTENTS

CHAPTER ONE

FOOTY PHENOM

Hi there. I'm Gary the G.O.A.T.

I may not be the **Greatest. Of. All. Time,** but I do have a winning streak in sports trivia!

Just call me **G-GOAT (Greatest Grandmaster Of Athletic Things).**

But you know who *is* an actual

HONEST-TO-GOODNESS

LEGEND?

Footy player

MARCUS BONTEMPELLI

And this book
is all about him!

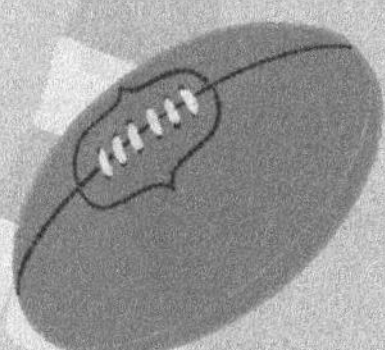

Marcus is an

and is considered one of the **best midfielders** in the **AFL.**

ON THE FIELD, he's famous for his **leadership and composure** under pressure. His clean skills and **precision kicking** make him one of the **game's greatest.**

OFF THE FIELD, he's **humble, hard-working,** and **respected** by teammates and fans alike. He leads with **confidence** and **always puts the team first.**

WHAT MAKES MARCUS SUCH A LEGEND ON THE FIELD?

SUPER SPEED & QUICK MOVES

Marcus is **fast** and can **change direction in a flash!** This helps him **chase the ball, dodge opponents** and make **quick decisions.**

STAMINA FOR DAAAAYS

Footy games are **long,** but Marcus has the **energy** to keep going from the **first bounce** to the **final siren.**

COOL UNDER PRESSURE

Even in a **tough game,** Marcus stays **calm** and **focused.** He doesn't let **nerves** get in the way of making **smart choices.**

BALL-HANDLING SKILLS

Marcus is great at **kicking the ball exactly where it needs to go,** and he can catch **tricky passes,** scoop up the ball off the ground and **handball** to a teammate in the blink of an eye.

TACTICAL AWARENESS

He knows where to **run,** when to **pass,** how to **find space** where there isn't any, and how to **set up big plays.**

VERSATILITY

Marcus can play in **different positions,** whether it's **midfield, forward,** or even helping in **defence.** No matter where he is, **he plays his best every time!**

MARCUS'S
LEGENDARY
SKILLS:
Endurance
Quick reflexes
Marking
Tackling and bumping
Running
Handballs and bouncing
Kicking

'Marcus is the prototype modern AFL midfielder; **tall** and **explosive** with **exquisite skills** to match.'

PATRICK DANGERFIELD,

captain of Geelong FC

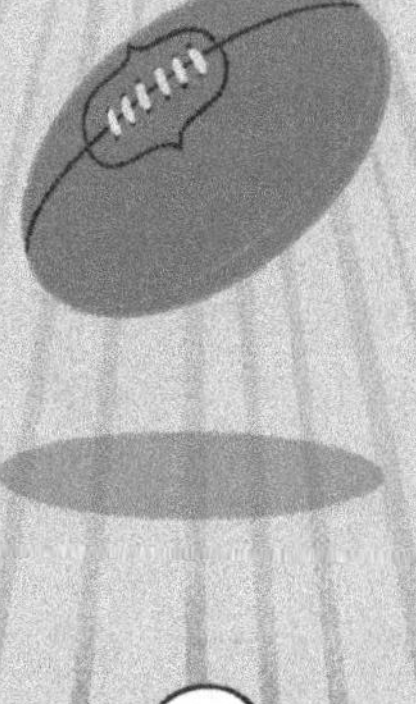

Name:
Marcus Bontempelli

Date of Birth:
24 November 1995

Place of Birth:
Melbourne, VIC
(Naarm, Kulin Nation)

Height:
1.94m

Number:
4

Position:
Midfielder/
forward

Nicknames:
The Bont,
Bonti

Clubs: Northern Knights, Eltham Panthers Football Club

Current AFL club: Western Bulldogs

CHAPTER TWO

THE FIRST BOUNCE

Marcus was born in **Melbourne/Naarm** and grew up in the **northern suburb of Eltham.**

Eltham is famous for **Montsalvat, Australia's oldest continuous artist community**. It was set up in **1934** and designed to look like a **medieval** (but charming) **French village.** There are over **2000 pieces of art** onsite!

Marcus is the son of **Carlo** and **Geraldine Bontempelli.** He has **three sisters,** Alanna, Olivia and Sienna, so his house was always full of **noise, fun** and **action.**

'As the only boy in my family, I had **no say** in what **after-school TV show** we'd watch and **hardly any buy-in** from my three sisters. So I spent hours by myself **playing** and **commentating.**'

MARCUS BONTEMPELLI

Marcus also has a **famous footy connection** – his cousin, **Nick Dal Santo,** played in the **AFL** too! He played for **St Kilda FC** and **North Melbourne FC.**

In his final year at **Marcellin College,** Marcus was the **sports captain** and played for both the **1st XVIII football team** and the **1st basketball team.**

He helped his school win two **basketball premierships,** became a **National School Boys basketball champion,** and played at club representative level for the **Eltham Wildcats Basketball Club.**

Even though he loved basketball, **footy was his true passion,** and it wasn't long before he had to choose one sport to focus on.

Lucky for AFL fans, he picked footy!

Marcus started out playing **junior footy** for the

where he showed off his **skills** as a **defender** and sometimes a sneaky **goal-kicker** up forward.

In **2013,** Marcus joined the

in the **TAC Cup,** playing against some of the **best young players** in **Victoria.** At first, he played as a **defender** and **forward,** but when he moved into the **midfield,** his game went to **another level!**

He participated in **19 games** and kicked **138 goals** throughout that season, AND he was selected to be in the **TAC Cup Team of the Year** on the **interchange bench.**

Marcus also played for **Victoria Metro** in the **2013 Under 18 Championships.**

'It was only the **final year of school** where things were being written about me and I started attracting attention. It took me a while to find my **confidence in sport,** and that's given me a better **appreciation** for what I have now.'

MARCUS BONTEMPELLI

‘I started to really play **consistently** through the **midfield,** that’s where I played **my best footy.**’

MARCUS BONTEMPELLI

With all this **talent** and **hard work,** it wasn’t long before **AFL clubs** started to take notice...

CHAPTER THREE

DRAFT DAY DREAMS

The end of 2013 was **exciting** for Marcus because that was the year he could be **drafted** to play in the

AUSTRALIAN FOOTBALL LEAGUE (AFL)!

The **AFL Draft** is a **big event** where **AFL clubs** get to pick the best young **unsigned players** to join their teams!

It happens **every November,** so that young players have time to **finish school** before starting their **AFL journey.**

REMEMBER!

The sport =
AUSTRALIAN RULES FOOTBALL

The main competition of that sport =
THE AUSTRALIAN FOOTBALL LEAGUE (AFL)

How does the

The teams that **finish lower** on the ladder get the **earliest picks,** so they have the **best chance** to select **top young talent.**

Each club **takes turns choosing players,** just like picking teams at school!

AFL draft work?

Once a player is picked, they **officially join that AFL club** and start **training** for the new season.

Generally, the **most promising players** are selected within the **earliest picks.**

Key Rules for the AFL Draft

AGE REQUIREMENT: Players must be at least **18 years old** by the end of the draft year.

ACADEMY & NEXT GENERATION PLAYERS: Some teams have special access to young players from their **zones** or **multicultural backgrounds.**

FATHER-SON RULE:

If a player's **dad** played **over 100 games** for an **AFL team,** that team gets the chance to draft them before others. (There is also a **Father-Daughter rule** for AFL Women's players!)

PRIORITY PICKS:

Teams that have **struggled** for a long time may get **extra picks** to help them **rebuild.**

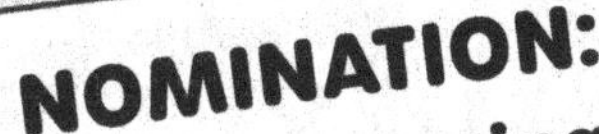

NOMINATION:

Players must **nominate for the draft** to be selected.

Before **the draft,** no one was quite sure where Marcus would end up. Some **experts** thought he'd be **picked early,** while others thought he might go as late as **pick 15!**

There were even **rumours** that

wanted to **trade** for him, but in the end, the

made the **big call** and...

Fun fact: Marcus was draft pick number four and also wears the number four!

'[I feel] **on top of the world** really, I guess my **dream of being an AFL player has just come true.** I am so **grateful for the Doggies** who have given me the opportunity to be their pick four and their **first pick.**'

MARCUS BONTEMPELLI

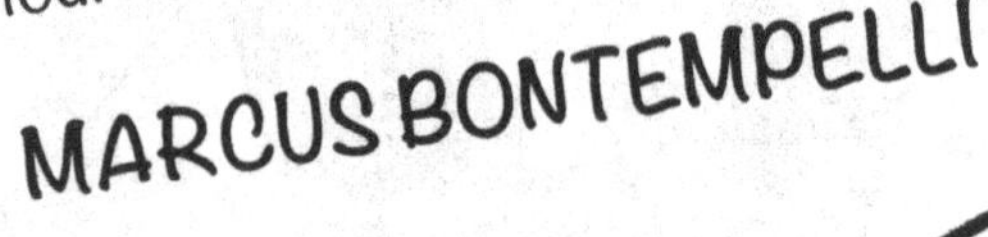

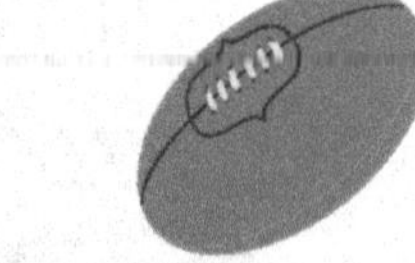

CHAPTER FOUR

A BULLDOG IS BORN

LEGENDARY GAME

WHO?

Western Bulldogs v Carlton Blues

WHAT?

Round 5, 2014 AFL season

WHERE?

Marvel Stadium, Melbourne

WHY WAS IT LEGENDARY?

Marcus made his **senior debut** for the **Western Bulldogs** in the **2014 season** and quickly **made his mark!** He played his **first game** in **Round 5** against **Carlton,** and though the Bulldogs lost by 28 points, Marcus collected **14 disposals** and **five tackles.**

'Running out for my first game was just a surreal moment. It's what I've been dreaming of and what I've been praying for.'

MARCUS BONTEMPELLI

20 April – a DOGGIE DEBUT to remember!

By **Round 13,** Marcus was **turning heads,** collecting **22 disposals** and **kicking a goal in a big win** over **Collingwood.**

That **performance** earned him a

proving he was one of the **best young players** in the **competition!**

LEGENDARY GAME

WHO?

Western Bulldogs v
Melbourne Demons

WHAT?

Round 15,
2014 AFL season

WHERE?

Marvel Stadium,
Melbourne

Why was it legendary?

Then came **Round 15.** The **Bulldogs** started well, but the **Demons tied the score** by the fourth quarter. With minutes left on the clock, **Marcus kicked an unbelievable goal from the boundary** to help his team snatch a **one-goal victory** over **Melbourne!**

By the **end of the year,**
Marcus had won the

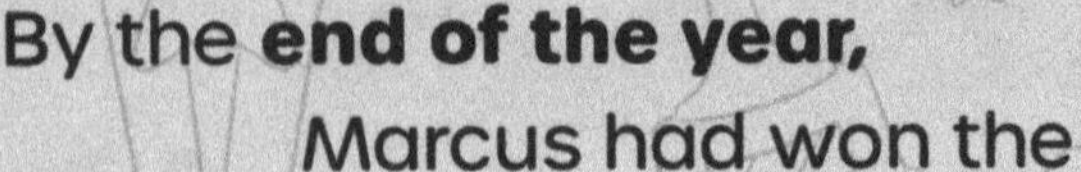

CHRIS GRANT BEST FIRST-YEAR PLAYER AWARD

for **the Bulldogs** and
was also named the

AFLPA BEST FIRST-YEAR PLAYER

He **missed out** on winning the **AFL Rising Star award,** finishing **second** by **just one vote.**

But it was clear…

THE BONT HAD ARRIVED!

Marcus **wasn't slowing down** in **2015!** He played almost every game, except for two when he was **out with an injury.**

He kept **improving,** and in a game against **Gold Coast,** he had a **career-high 28 disposals, kicked two goals** and **laid seven tackles!**

He also played in the Bulldogs' **first final in five years,** picking up **24 disposals** and **seven tackles** in a **nail-biting elimination final** against **Adelaide.** Even though the Bulldogs lost by just seven points, Marcus was **one of their best players** on the day.

By the end of the 2015 season, Marcus had . . .

Finished third in the **BULLDOGS' BEST & FAIREST** (behind **Easton Wood** and **Bob Murphy**).

More than tripled his **Brownlow votes** from his first year, leading the Bulldogs with **13 votes** at just **19 years old!**

Earned four 'best on ground' performances (including **back-to-back** in the first two rounds!).

Been selected in the **22 Under 22 team** for the **second year in a row.**

Climbed up the **AFL Player Ratings** to sit **eleventh overall** in the **AFL,** becoming the **youngest player ever** to feature in the **top 20!**

'I think his **teammates look up to him** already, which – for a second-year player – is a **great effort.** We've only tapped the surface of what Marcus can produce as a player.'

STEVEN KING,
midfield coach, Western Bulldogs

With all this **success,** the Bulldogs knew they had a **FUTURE SUPERSTAR.** In September 2015, Marcus **signed a long-term contract** to stay at the **'Kennel'** until 2019.

CHAPTER FIVE

GRAND FINAL GLORY

The **2016 season** was Marcus's **BEST YET** – and a year that Bulldogs fans will **never forget!**

He played EVERY GAME in the season.

He kicked the FIRST GOAL of the season 20 SECONDS into the game against the FREMANTLE DOCKERS.

He helped lead the Bulldogs to a HISTORIC PREMIERSHIP VICTORY!

'I wanted to achieve some **consistency** (this year) and become a player that was **able to turn up week in, week out.** On-field it was just about **playing good footy** for as long as I could and helping get this team across the line.'
MARCUS BONTEMPELLI

Marcus had joined the Bulldogs' **leadership group** at the start of the year. He even **filled in as captain** for a game against the

WEST COAST EAGLES

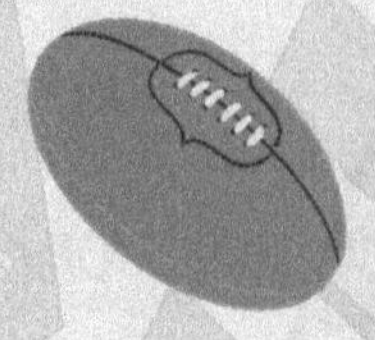

becoming the **youngest player ever** to lead a team to **victory!**

In Round 8, he had a **career-high 33 disposals** against the **Melbourne Demons,** showing he was one of the league's **RISING STARS.**

But the real magic came in the finals . . .

LEGENDARY GAME

WHO?
Western Bulldogs v Sydney Swans

WHAT?
2016 AFL Grand Final

WHERE?
Melbourne Cricket Ground (MCG)

WHY WAS IT LEGENDARY?
The Bulldogs **defied the odds,** winning **four knockout finals in a row** to make it to their **first Grand Final since 1954!** After a thrilling game against Sydney, the Bulldogs claimed the **AFL premiership, winning by 22 points** with a **89-67 victory** over the **Swans.**

Fairytale Finish

After waiting **62 years** for another flag, the Bulldogs' **fans went wild!** It was a moment in **footy history,** and **the Bont was at the heart of it!**

'This group of players are just **incredible.** Their **hearts are so big.**'

LUKE BEVERIDGE, senior coach, Western Bulldogs

'It's been such a **long wait** for the fans and everyone at the club, it's just **unreal.** You never want to think you won, but I looked to the bench and saw that **everyone was in tears and hugging each other** so I thought it was probably **time for me to start celebrating as well.**'

LACHIE HUNTER,
Western Bulldogs

The **Western Bulldogs** were also the **first team** to ever **win the AFL flag** after finishing **seventh** on the ladder.

99,981 spectators attended the final at **the MCG.** The MCG capacity is **just over 100,000.** Talk about a crowd!

Bontempelli was one of **THE STARS** of the game. His **incredible season** earned him…

- the **Charles Sutton Medal** (for the Bulldogs' **Best & Fairest**)

- a spot on the **All-Australian team** for the first time

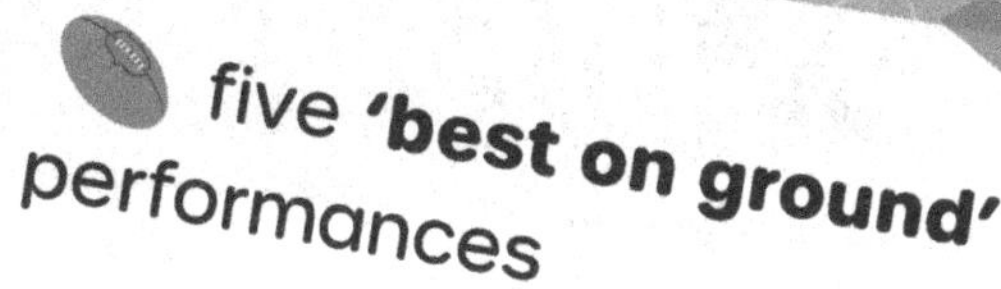

captain of the **22 Under 22 Team**

AFL club supported as a kid:
Richmond

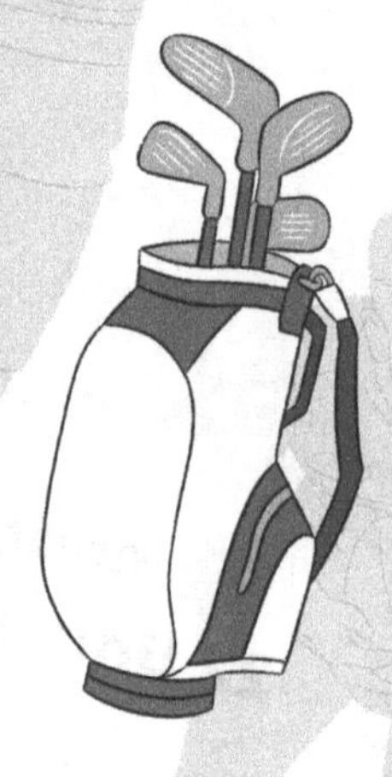

Before a game I always:
Walk and listen to music

All-time favourite player:
Matthew Richardson

On my days off, I like to:
Watch a movie, relax, spend time with family, play golf

Childhood hero:
Red Power Ranger

Least preferred household chore:
Taking the bins out

Favourite professional sporting team:
Chicago Bulls

Favourite sporting hero:
Roger Federer

Guilty pleasure:
Choc mint ice-cream

Favourite cartoon:
Dragon Ball Z

Favourite holiday spot:
New York

If I wasn't a footballer I'd be...
A basketballer

Best advice I've received:
You make your own luck

CHAPTER SIX

FOOTY FACTS

AUSTRALIAN RULES FOOTBALL is one of the most **exciting** and **fast-paced** sports in the country!

The **AUSTRALIAN FOOTBALL LEAGUE (AFL)** is the **biggest professional competition** of Australian rules football.

Think of **Aussie Rules** as a mix of soccer, rugby and basketball – only **faster** and **more thrilling!**

DID YOU KNOW,
Carlton, Collingwood and Essendon have won the **most premierships** so far? Each club has won **16 each!**

There are **23 rounds of games in an AFL premiership season.** The **top eight teams** make the **Finals Series,** and the last two teams standing face off in the **AFL Grand Final** at the **MCG!**

THE BASICS

SHAPE:
Oval (like a giant egg!)

SIZE:
Around 135–185m long and 110–155m wide – bigger than two soccer fields!

ZONES:

- **Centre Square** – where the action starts
- **Forward 50** – where teams try to score
- **Defensive 50** – where teams stop the other side from scoring

THE BALL

Made of leather, and oval-shaped

Usually red-coloured for day games or yellow-coloured for night games (yellow is more popular because it's easier to see!)

THE PLAYERS

18 players per team on the field

4 interchange (bench) players who swap in and out

Players wear guernseys/ jumpers, shorts and boots with studs for grip

HOW THE GAME WORKS

STARTING THE GAME

- The **umpire bounces the ball** in the **centre** of the field
- Players jump up and **tap the ball** to their teammates

MOVING THE BALL

- **KICKING** – the most powerful way to pass!
- **HANDBALLING** – punching the ball to a teammate
- **RUNNING WITH THE BALL** – but you must bounce it every 15 metres
- **TACKLING** – you can tackle an opponent if they have the ball, but no high tackles! (Above the shoulders = free kick for the other team!)
- **MARKING** – if you catch the ball from a kick over 15 metres, you get a free kick

SCORING

The aim is to **kick the ball** through the **goalposts!**

- **GOAL (6 POINTS):** Kick the ball between the two tall posts without anyone touching it
- **BEHIND (1 POINT):** If the ball goes between the smaller posts or is touched before crossing the goal line

EXAMPLE SCORE:

Western Bulldogs 12.10 (82) defeated Sydney Swans 9.7 (61)

- **The first number** = Goals
- **The second number** = Behinds
- **The number in brackets** = Total Score!

THE FIELD

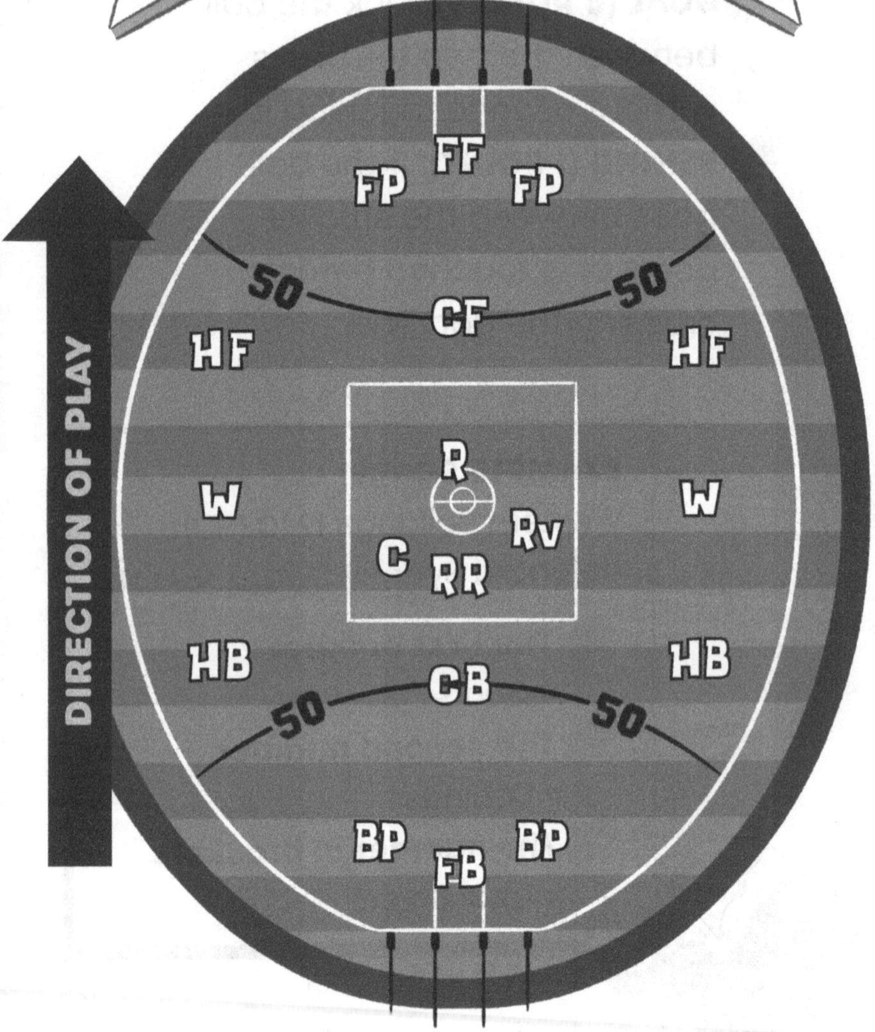

FF

FP FP

50 50

CF

HF HF

R

W W

Rv

C RR

HB HB

CB

50 50

BP BP

FB

DIRECTION OF PLAY

FORWARDS (SCORE GOALS!)

Full Forward: The main goal kicker
Forward Pockets: Helps the full forward and snaps quick goals
Half-Forward Flanks: Links the midfield and forwards and sets up attacks
Centre Half-Forward: A key attacker who takes big marks and kicks goals

MIDFIELDERS (CONTROL THE GAME!)

Centre: Wins clearances, starts plays and moves the ball forward
Wingmen: Moves up and down the flanks, linking defence to attack
Ruckman: The tallest player who taps the ball from throw-ins and bounces
Ruck Rover: Supports the ruckman and gets the ball moving
Rover: A small, fast player who wins the ball at ground level

DEFENDERS (PROTECT THE GOAL!)

Full Back: Defends against the opposition's main goal kicker
Back Pockets: Helps clear the ball from the defensive area
Half-Back Flanks: Intercepts the ball and start counter-attacks
Centre Half-Back: A key defender who shuts down big forwards

A GAME WITH A

Aussie Rules started in **1858** in **Victoria,** making it one of the world's **oldest** football games.

Cricketers invented it! It was created as a way to **keep cricketers fit** during the winter.

The very **first game** was played in **1858** between two schools – **Melbourne Grammar** and **Scotch College.**

Melbourne and **Geelong** were the **first footy clubs,** and they're still playing today!

AFLW launched in 2017! Women's footy is now bigger than ever, with **thousands of girls** playing across the country.

LONG HISTORY!

The game spread fast, and by **1897,** the **Victorian Football League (VFL)** was formed. As teams from all over Australia joined, the league changed its name to the **Australian Football League (AFL)** in **1990.**

The **AFL Grand Final** is the **second-highest-attended club championship event** in the world.

The **MCG** is the **largest ground** in the AFL, with a **capacity of 100,024.** The **smallest ground** is **Riverway Stadium** in Queensland, with a **capacity of just 10,000.**

TEAMS

Currently, 18 TEAMS from Victoria, New South Wales, Queensland, South Australia and Western Australia compete in the league. Each team has a THEME SONG they sing when they win!

Adelaide Crows
Brisbane Lions
Carlton Blues
Collingwood Magpies
Essendon Bombers
Fremantle Dockers
Geelong Cats
Gold Coast Suns
Greater Western Sydney Giants
Hawthorn Hawks
Melbourne Demons
North Melbourne Kangaroos
Port Adelaide Power
Richmond Tigers
St Kilda Saints
Sydney Swans
West Coast Eagles
Western Bulldogs

MARN GROOK

It's possible the game was around before 1858 in a **different format!**

Aussie Rules Football might have been **influenced by Marn Grook,** a ball game played by **Indigenous communities** around Australia for **centuries.**

It involves **kicking, catching** and **leaping high to grab the ball** – just like in **Aussie Rules!**

Unlike Aussie Rules, Marn Grook can have more than 100 players on the field!

CHAPTER SEVEN

RISING STAR

Marcus started 2017 with an **ankle injury,** but once the season kicked off, he was **unstoppable!**

He played **two of his best games** against **Carlton** and **Sydney,** and by the end of the season, he led the Bulldogs in **tackles, clearances, contested marks** and more!

At the end of the year, the Bulldogs made a **big decision.** With captain **Bob Murphy** retiring and vice-captain **Easton Wood** being promoted, they needed a **new vice-captain.**

Marcus played **almost every game in 2018.** But in July, something unexpected happened – he had **appendicitis!**

Appendicitis is when your appendix becomes inflamed. Doctors need to take it out quickly when this happens!

He needed **emergency surgery** and had to miss a **VERY SPECIAL round 7 match** that would have been his **100th game.**

When he finally played his

in round 19, he picked up **22 disposals** against **Port Adelaide.** Sadly, the Bulldogs lost the game.

But **the Bont kept improving.** He broke his **personal record** for the **most disposals in a game - twice in a row!** Then, he became the first player ever to make the **22 Under 22 team five years in a row!**

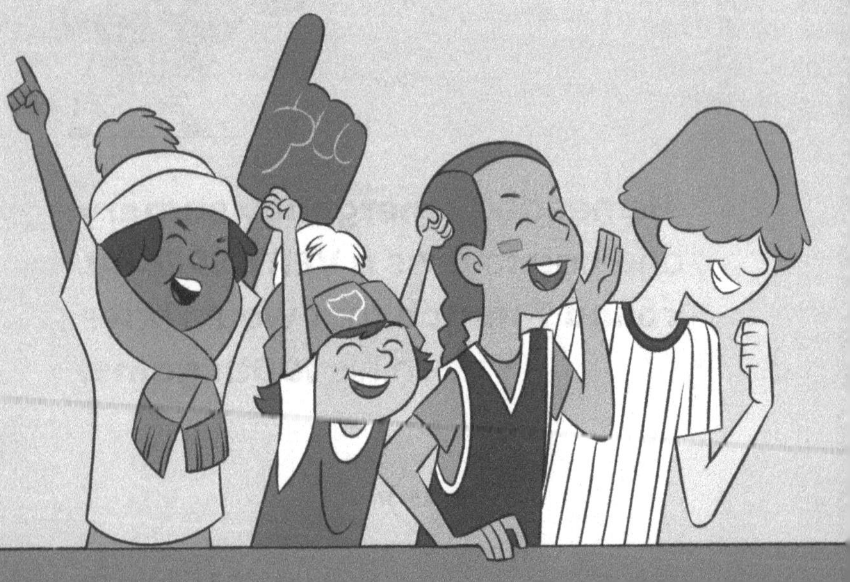

Though it was a **tough year,** Marcus was keen to stick around **the Kennel.** In November, he signed a **three-year contract extension.**

2019 WAS EVEN BIGGER!

Marcus helped lead the Bulldogs **back to the finals** and had **five games with 30 or more disposals.** One of his **best performances** was against **Richmond** in round 7, where he had **27 disposals** and **kicked three goals!**

He was so good this season, he won the **AFL Coaches Association Player of the Year award** – the first Bulldog ever to do it!

'He may go down as their **greatest ever player** at the Western Bulldogs.'

MATTHEW LLOYD,
Essendon Bombers veteran

At the end of 2019, **Easton Wood stepped down as captain.** The Bulldogs needed a **new leader,** and they had the **perfect choice.**

MARCUS BONTEMPELLI was named the club's new captain!

'When I stood down from captaincy, I knew **Marcus would be ready.** He's the **best example** to follow in our football club, by far.'

EASTON WOOD,
Western Bulldogs veteran and former captain

CHAPTER EIGHT

LEADING FROM THE FRONT

The **2020 season** was a **tough one,** but Marcus showed **exceptional leadership skills.**

His first year as **skipper** saw him selected for the **All-Australian team** for the **third time** and he led his team to the **finals again.**

AND he won the **Scott West Most Courageous Player Award.**

‘It was clear that the **best thing for our football club was for Marcus to be leading it.** He couldn’t have taken over at a more **difficult time,** head-on into a **pandemic.** But he’s attacked the **captaincy** in the same way he’s attacked his football. He’s **curious** about how to get better, he **explores,** he works on it, and **he’s all-in.**’

EASTON WOOD,
Western Bulldogs veteran
and former captain

In 2021, Marcus reached

NEW HEIGHTS!

He played his

and kept **leading the team** with **amazing performances,** including **four goals** in a **111-point win** over **St Kilda** in **round 10!**

Marcus was a **favourite** to win the **prestigious Brownlow Medal,** but unfortunately he finished **second.** However, he was named

AFLPA's BEST CAPTAIN

and he **won his fourth**

LEGENDARY GAME

WHO?
Western Bulldogs v
Melbourne Demons

WHAT?
2021 AFL Grand Final

WHERE?
Optus Stadium, Perth

WHY WAS IT LEGENDARY?

In 2021, the Bulldogs were in the **GRAND FINAL** again. Marcus was **kicking goals,** and at one point, they were **up by 19 points!** But in the last quarter, the Demons completely turned the game around in their favour and took home the victory...

WESTERN BULLDOGS
WESTERN BULLDOGS
WESTERN BULLDOGS
WESTERN BULLDOGS
WESTERN BULLDOGS
'We'll get **another chance,** hopefully, to play football again and **resurrect** some of the things that we didn't do well. You've just got to **look forward to the future and be positive** about it.'
MARCUS BONTEMPELLI
4

2022 was full of **injuries** and **challenges** for Marcus and the Western Bulldogs.

He was **sidelined** for a while after **catching the flu,** then he suffered an **adductor injury,** but Marcus continued to **inspire** his team as much as he could.

But 2023 was the

OPPOSITE!

Marcus won his **fifth Charles Sutton Medal,** finished **second in the Brownlow Medal (again!),** and was also **second in the AFL Coaches Association's Player of the Year award.**

LEGENDARY GAME

WHO?

Western Bulldogs v
Hawthorn Hawks

WHAT?

Round 7, 2023 AFL Season

WHERE?

Marvel Stadium, Melbourne

WHY WAS IT LEGENDARY?

In 2023, Marcus celebrated his **200th AFL game** with a **29-point win over Hawthorn Hawks!!!** The Hawks took the lead in the first half, but the Bulldogs pushed back and claimed the win. Marcus didn't kick any goals, but he picked up **20 disposals** and a **HUGE milestone!**

‘We’re **really fortunate** to have him, he’s an **exceptional human being.** It’s a big occasion and hopefully we can **show our best** and then **celebrate his milestone** after the game.’

LUKE BEVERIDGE,
senior coach, Western Bulldogs

The **2024 season** was full of **more wins** for **the Bont:**

Though he **missed out** on a premiership and the Brownlow medal in 2024, it's clear that **Marcus has plenty more footy to play!**

CHAPTER NINE

BEST ON GROUND

Marcus has **achieved A LOT** throughout his

with the **Western Bulldogs.** He's been compared to some of the **greatest players in the game,** and many believe he will go down as the **best Bulldog of all time.**

On top of that, he **widely admired** and **well-liked** by fans, teammates and the broader AFL community. He is...

An Outstanding Player

A Respected Captain

A Team & Fan Favourite

Humble & Hardworking

A Great Role Model

Let's take a look at some of these **achievements** and hear from people who know him!

TEAM ACHIEVEMENTS

AFL PREMIERSHIP PLAYER: 2016, contributing significantly to the Bulldogs' first premiership in 62 years

INDIVIDUAL HONOURS

WESTERN BULLDOGS CAPTAIN: 2020–present, demonstrating leadership and commitment to the team

LEIGH MATTHEWS TROPHY (AFLPA MOST VALUABLE PLAYER): Three-time recipient in 2021, 2023 and 2024, reflecting peer recognition of his outstanding performance

ALL-AUSTRALIAN TEAM SELECTIONS: Six-time honouree in 2016, 2019, 2020, 2021 (vice-captain), 2023 (vice-captain) and 2024 (captain), showcasing consistent elite performance

CHARLES SUTTON MEDAL (WESTERN BULLDOGS BEST AND FAIREST): Six-time winner in 2016, 2017, 2019, 2021, 2023 and 2024, highlighting his value to the club

AFLPA BEST CAPTAIN AWARD: Three-time recipient in 2021, 2023, and 2024, for his leadership qualities

'He's got **great values.** He's **respectful** and very **humble** but he's also pretty **driven** and **determined** for not only himself but the club.'

STEVEN KING,
midfield coach,
Western Bulldogs

'Right from the get-go I think the thing that stood out was his **work ethic** and his **willingness to take feedback** on and **work on his game.**'

MATTHEW BOYD,
Western Bulldogs veteran

INDIVIDUAL HONOURS

BRUCE WILKINSON WINNER (AFL TRAINERS' AWARD): 2021, awarded by the club's medical and training team in recognition of his **commitment to peak performance** throughout the season

DOUG HAWKINS MEDAL: 2020, the second-place medal for the Western Bulldogs **Best and Fairest** vote count

JOHN VAN GRONINGEN COOLUM NINDERRY AWARD: Four-time winner in 2019, 2021, 2023 and 2024, voted for by the players and coaches for his **leadership and team-first approach**

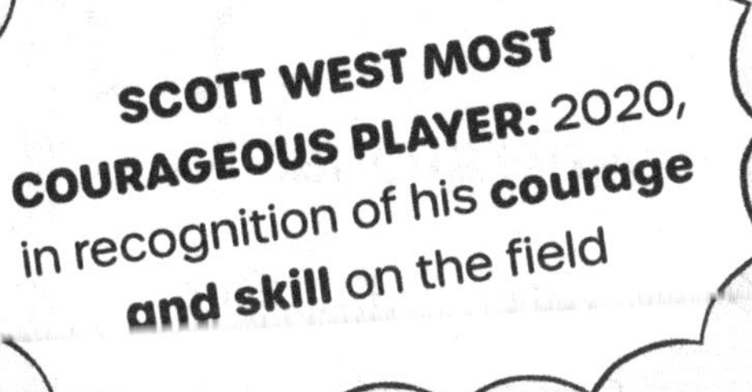

SCOTT WEST MOST COURAGEOUS PLAYER: 2020, in recognition of his **courage and skill** on the field

AFLCA CHAMPION PLAYER OF THE YEAR AWARD: 2019, acknowledging his **excellence** as judged by coaches

GARY DEMPSEY MEDAL: 2015 and 2018, the third-place medal for the Western Bulldogs **Best and Fairest** vote count

'He's a **generational** kind of player and teammate. He came to us when the club was in a pretty dark spot, and sometimes the **universe delivers a little gift.** We felt that way with Marcus.'

BOB MURPHY,
Western Bulldogs veteran and former captain

He's an **extraordinary talent,** this bloke. He could well end up being the **best player the club's ever had** – even greater than the great **EJ Whitten.'**

GERARD HEALY,
AFL veteran and
former commentator

INDIVIDUAL HONOURS

AFLCA BEST YOUNG PLAYER OF THE YEAR: 2015, highlighting his early career promise

AFLPA BEST FIRST-YEAR PLAYER: 2014, recognising his immediate impact in his debut season

AFL RISING STAR NOMINEE: 2014, marking his emergence as a talented newcomer

CHRIS GRANT BEST FIRST-YEAR PLAYER: 2014, given to a Western Bulldogs player who has had a standout first season.

AFLPA 22UNDER22 TEAM SELECTIONS: Five-time member from 2014 to 2018, serving as captain from 2016 to 2018, reflecting his status among the best young players

All that's missing is a Brownlow Medal!

'He's playing some **very influential footy**... we use that term **'match-winner'** sparingly and it's a label that he can definitely have in brackets after his name because **he's that kind of player.'**

LUKE BEVERIDGE,
senior coach, Western Bulldogs

'There's a point in your **career** where you go from being a **player for the Bulldogs** to a **player of the Bulldogs.** Marcus had that **epiphany** early, and he continues to drive that. He **cares so deeply** for this club.'

EASTON WOOD,
Western Bulldogs veteran and former captain

'I get an **enormous amount of support and help** from a lot of people, but I think I'm **lucky** that the environment I'm in allows me to **stay curious** and try to be **the best influence** I can be for the football club.'

MARCUS BONTEMPELLI

CHAPTER TEN

THE BONT

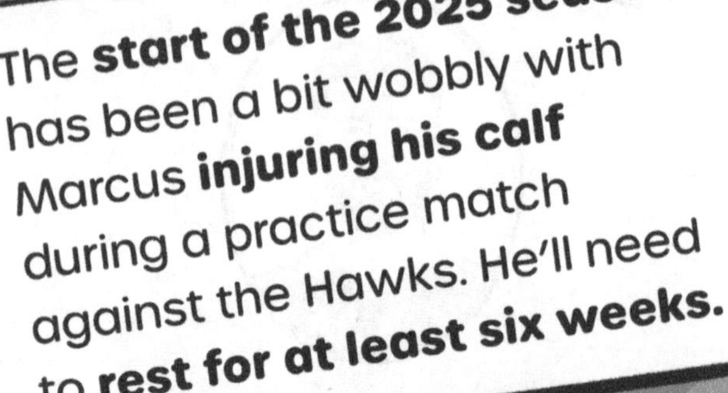
The **start of the 2025 season** has been a bit wobbly with Marcus **injuring his calf** during a practice match against the Hawks. He'll need to **rest for at least six weeks.**

'Yeah, I will be alright.'
MARCUS BONTEMPELLI

But, as we know, **anything can happen,** and this could be the year the Bulldogs **win another premiership!**

'They're a **massive chance to win the premiership, the Dogs.** I love their **pressure** around the ball. I love the fact they are working really hard **defensively** and **offensively.**'

PAUL ROOS,
former AFL coach

Things The

His nonna

Lasagna

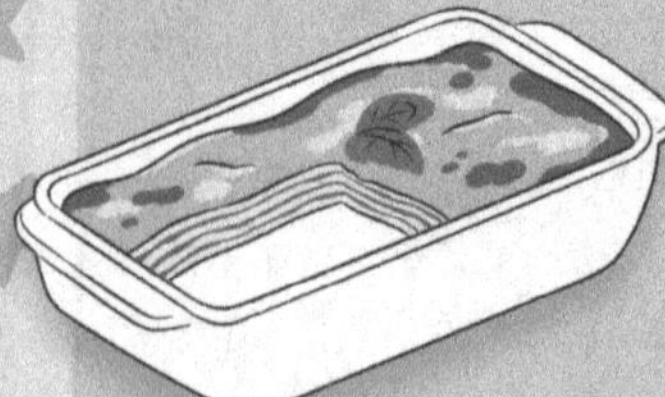

His dog, Mya

Watching movies

Spending time with family

BONT loves

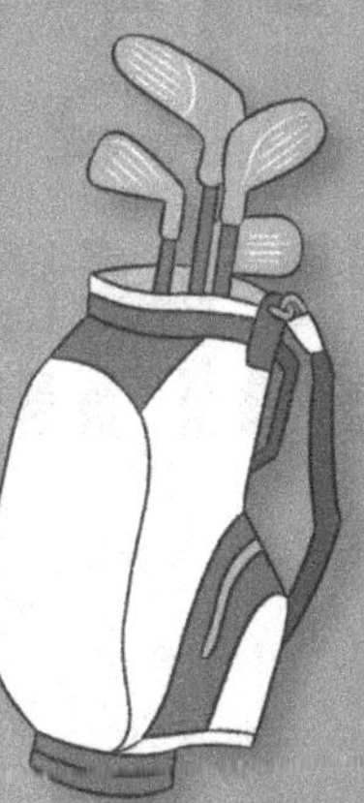

Marcus **cares deeply about important issues** and uses his voice to **make a difference.**

In 2015, he teamed up with fellow AFL stars **Shaun Burgoyne** and **Patrick Dangerfield** to **take a stand against violence towards women** as part of the

THROUGH THE LINE CAMPAIGN.

'For us as AFL players, [we need] to be able to **produce the right message for kids and young people** growing up, that it's **not okay to cross the line when it comes to women.'**

MARCUS BONTEMPELLI

Growing up with **strong women** in his life, Marcus has always respected their influence. That's why he supports **THE LINE,** a program that **teaches kids about respect and healthy relationships.**

Marcus also **loves helping young people.**

He's volunteered for **LADDER,** a charity where **AFL players mentor and support kids in need,** and he's also an ambassador for **MY ROOM,** working hard to raise **awareness** and **funds** to help **fight childhood cancer.**

Plus, in 2017, he spoke up for **marriage equality,** saying it would make a **big difference** for many people.

THE LEGENDARY MARCUS BONTEMPELLI

232 CAREER GOALS

190 CAREER BEHINDS

6 TIME ALL-AUSTRALIAN

No doubt about it,

Marcus Bontempelli

is a true

SPORTING LEGEND!

1. In what Australian city was Marcus born?
2. What number does Marcus wear on his guernsey?
3. How many players are on the field for each team during an AFL game?
4. What other sport did Marcus play growing up?

Baulk: when a player holds the ball out to the side in one hand, then runs in the other direction to evade a defender.

Pill: Another way of describing the footy.

Hospital kick/handball: A high, looping pass that puts the receiver in a vulnerable position to be tackled hard. Ouch!

Pine: Slang for the interchange bench where substitute players sit.

Rainmaker: A very high kick that seems to touch the sky! Unfortunately, it doesn't travel very far...

Smother: When you block an opponent's kick right off their boot.

Snap: A quick, short kick, usually executed under pressure and often while turning.

Woodwork: Refers to the goalposts - hitting the woodwork means the ball struck the post.

Coathanger: An illegal high tackle where a player's arm catches another player around the head or neck. Don't do this!